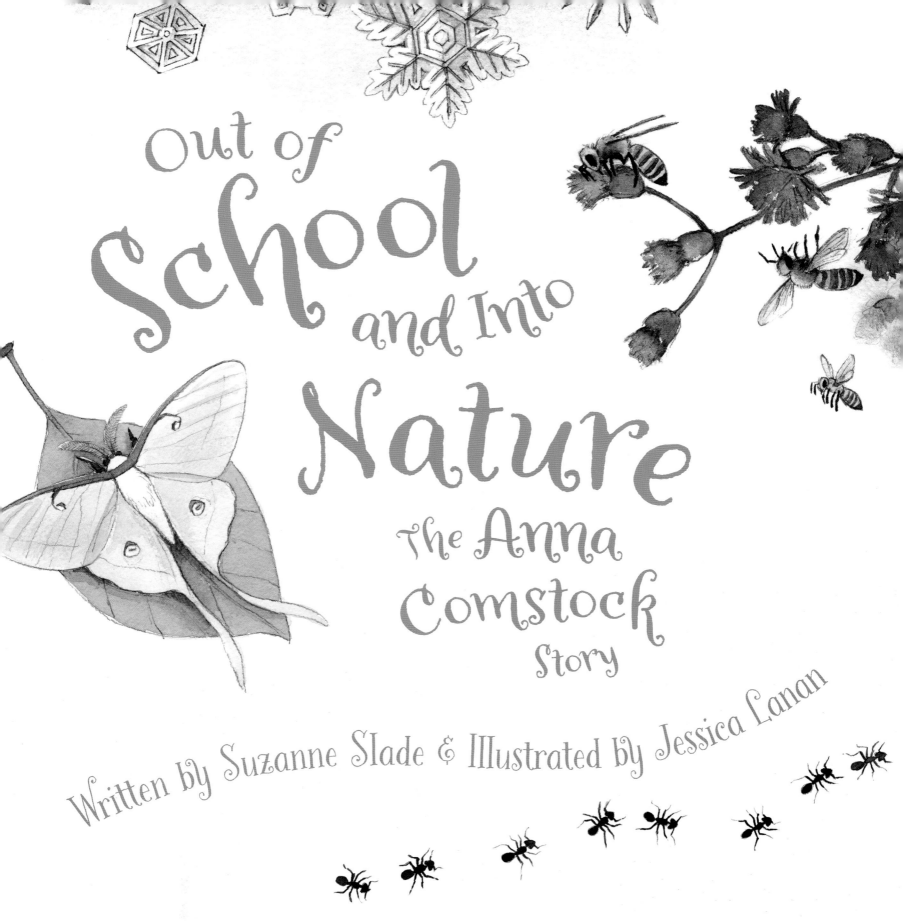

Out of School and Into Nature

The Anna Comstock Story

Written by Suzanne Slade & Illustrated by Jessica Lanan

From the time she was no higher than a daisy,
Anna was wild about nature.

She loved to hold it close in her fingers, she wanted to feel it squish between her toes, which was why she ran barefoot all summer long, raised slimy tadpoles into pet toads, and climbed tall trees instead of sitting in their shade.

Sometimes Anna just sat–watching.

"One of my joys was going barefoot
from early spring until late autumn."

That's how she discovered nature's secrets.

Leafy moths demonstrated the art of camouflage.

Fuzzy bees showed her pollination.

And marching ants explained all about teamwork.

Through the years Anna grew like a sunflower.
So did her love of nature.

Her mother taught her the names of wildflowers dancing in the meadow. At night, she whispered the names of the constellations twinkling in the velvety black sky.

Back then, girls were supposed to get married after high school. But Anna's heart belonged to her first love—nature. So she took off for college to learn more of its secrets. Anna studied plants and insects she'd never seen before.

"Such thousands of insects I never saw before!"

The more she learned, the more she wanted to share her discoveries.

So she began to draw.

Slowly. Carefully.

Her bugs looked so real they almost crawled right off the paper!

Amazed by her art, a professor started using her pictures during his lectures.

Farmers studied her detailed sketches to identify hungry bugs stealing their crops.

Yet Anna dreamed of creating even more realistic pictures. So she started carving fine lines into a block of wood. When she rolled ink over her engraving and pressed paper on top—MAGIC! A beautiful print appeared.

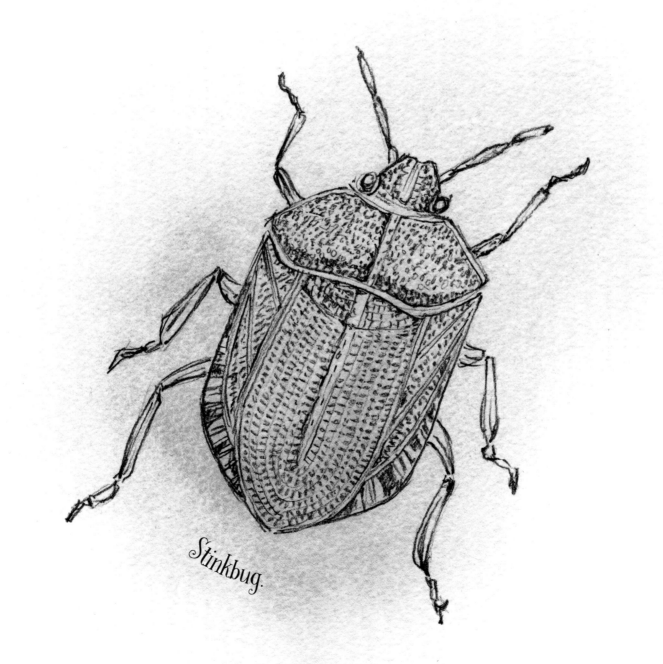

Stinkbug.

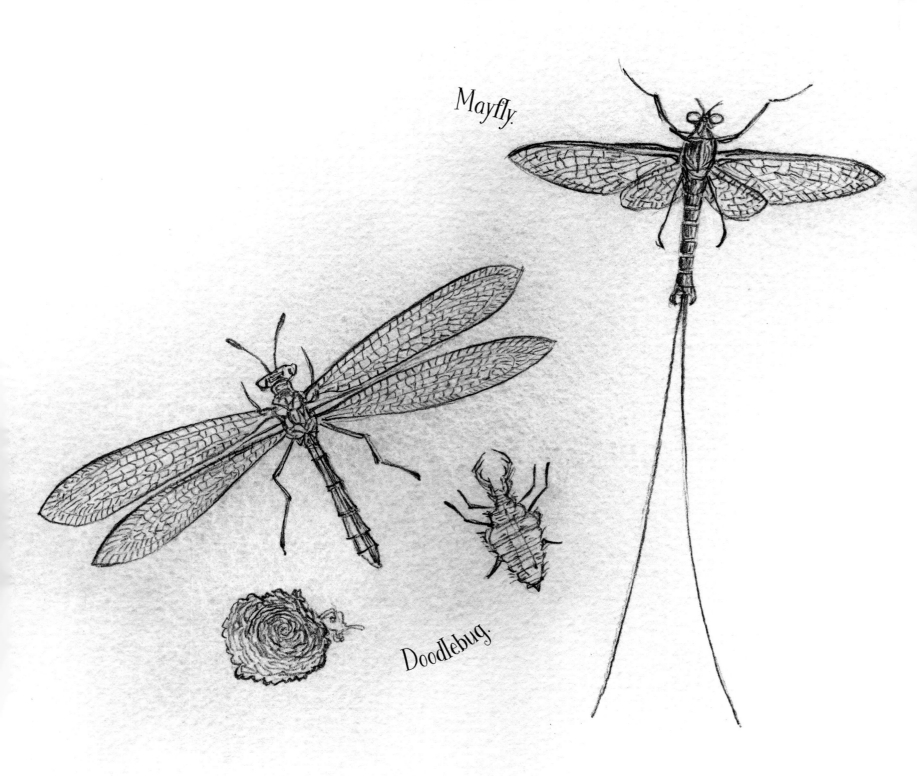

Mayfly.

Doodlebug.

Each one was breathtaking!

Anna was a fine artist. But she was a
scientist too. Peering through her microscope, she
studied delicate wings, legs, and antennae to create her art.

In her day most people thought men belonged in science—not women.
Anna thought they were as nutty as an oak tree. So she kept on
researching and drawing. She created illustrations for an insect book
so others could learn about these tiny creatures.

In time, she became a nature expert.

Then one day Anna made a surprising discovery.

While visiting nearby schools she realized they didn't have any nature classes. In fact, most New York schools weren't teaching about nature. It seemed other subjects were more "important," like reading, writing, and math. Anna knew this needed to change—and fast!

So she decided to start by teaching the teachers. Anna grabbed her pen and wrote lessons about nature's marvelous mysteries.

Caterpillars changing into graceful butterflies.

Water freezing into six-sided snowflakes.

Trees turning rain and sunlight into sweet sap.

Her lessons captivated curious teachers.
Soon, nature classes sprouted up in schools everywhere.

But Anna believed children should EXPERIENCE nature too. They needed to hold it close in their fingers, feel it squish between their toes. Then nature itself could teach children.

So Anna asked teachers to take their classes outside.

People thought she was crazy. Didn't she know school rules? Students learn inside. Students play outside!

Determined, Anna didn't give up. She wanted children to become passionate about wildlife—to take care of the environment.

"Nature study cultivates in the child a love of the beautiful."

Finally several schools agreed. Notebooks in hand, students tromped through forests and fields. Fascinated by the wonders around them, they stopped and sat—watching.

That's how they discovered nature's secrets.

Spiders spinning sticky webs.

Brown bats snoozing upside down.

Tadpoles sprouting stubby legs.

And the children became wild about nature!

News of Anna's outdoor study spread faster than dandelion seeds on a windy day. Soon classes across New York—across the country—headed outside.

Because Anna changed the rules, children realized how all living things are connected.

Unique. Important.

And they wanted to learn more.

So Anna decided to create books
about nature.

Year after year, she wrote.

She drew.

But she always made time for her first love—nature.

Anna held it close in her fingers,

felt it squish between her toes

until her very last days.

"The nature story is never finished. There is not a weed or an insect or a tree so common that the child, by observing carefully, may not see things never yet recorded."
—Anna Comstock

More About Anna

Known as the mother of nature education, Anna Botsford Comstock helped generations of children explore and fall in love with nature. She was also an important role model who boldly changed the "rules," proving that women could be researchers, scientists, and college professors. Among her many honors, Anna is one of only four women inducted into the National Wildlife Federation's Conservation Hall of Fame.®

Soon after Anna enrolled at Cornell University in 1874, she met a young professor named John Henry ("Harry") Comstock who was also crazy about nature. Impressed by his large insect collection, she eventually decided to marry that man, bugs and all. Together, the two created several books about insects. Harry wrote the words, while Anna created the drawings. After many years of research, studying, and drawing, Anna became a well-known nature expert.

In 1895, New York officials asked Anna for help when farms across the state began producing less food. The crop shortage started after farm children decided to move to cities when they grew up instead of staying to work the family fields. Fewer farm workers meant less food for everyone. But no one knew why the children had lost interest in farming—in nature. So state officials appointed Anna, along with twelve other experts, to the Committee for the Promotion of Agriculture to study the problem. When Anna set out to investigate, she discovered nearby schools weren't teaching about nature, which resulted in students who didn't appreciate the land, or farming. To help solve this problem, Anna decided to start

a nature-study program for teachers with Liberty Hyde Bailey, a Cornell professor. The program was so successful in New York, it grew into a nationwide teacher-education program. Soon, Anna began teaching nature-study classes for teachers at Cornell University. In 1898 she was appointed Assistant Professor of Nature Study, and became the first woman given the title "Professor" at Cornell.

Anna shared her passion for nature through her writing and art. Her engraved artwork was displayed at fine expositions in Paris, Chicago, and Buffalo, New York. She also wrote and/or illustrated nine nature books. Her most popular book, *Handbook of Nature Study*, contained lessons about a wide variety of topics: bugs and birds, fossils and flowers, soil and stars. She drew dozens of illustrations for the book and invited other experts to write a few lessons. When her huge book (over 900 pages!) was released in 1911, it flew off bookstore shelves like swallows soaring south in summer. Her book encouraged students to write and draw what they found in their own field notebooks, which she called "precious beyond price to their owners."

When Anna passed away in 1930, she didn't stop sharing her love of nature. Her beloved nature-study handbook has been translated into eight languages and reprinted dozens of times. Today children around the world still enjoy her book. Many of her readers have become nature teachers, keeping her passion for the environment alive.

To Rachel Hurd, who is passionate about improving schools and works
tirelessly to find the best ways to help each child learn.

—Suzanne

✲

To the entomologist in the family.

—Jessica

Author's Acknowledgment

With gratitude to Hilary Dorsch Wong (Reference Coordinator) and Eisha Neely (Exhibitions Coordinator & Reference Specialist)
from Division of Rare and Manuscript Collections, Cornell University, for their research assistance. And special thanks to
Prairie Crossing Charter School of Grayslake, Illinois, for inspiring me to write a book about Anna Comstock.

Quotes Sources

p. 5—"One of my . . . until late autumn." [*The Comstocks of Cornell*, p. 64]

p. 11—"Such thousands of . . . never saw before!" [*Comstocks of Cornell*, p. 85]

p. 23—"Nature study cultivates . . . of the beautiful." [*Handbook*, p. 1]

p. 30—"The nature story . . . never yet recorded." [*Handbook*, p. 11]

p. 31—"precious beyond price to their owners." [*Handbook*, p. 15]

Comstock, Anna Botsford. *The Comstocks of Cornell: John Henry Comstock and Anna Botsford Comstock*. Ithaca, New York:
Comstock Publishing Associates, 1953. Accessed through HathiTrust Digital Library. http://ittybittyurl.com/Yxy.

Comstock, Anna Botsford. *Handbook of Nature-Study*. Ithaca, New York: Comstock Publishing Associates, 1918.

Art from Anna Comstock's Engraving of Three Butterflies on page 31

John Henry and Anna Botsford Comstock papers, 21-23-25 box 17 folder 6.

Division of Rare and Manuscript Collections, Cornell University Library.

Sleeping Bear Press™

2395 South Huron Parkway, Suite 200
Ann Arbor, MI 48104
www.sleepingbearpress.com

Printed and bound in the United States.

10 9 8 7 6 5 4

Library of Congress Cataloging-in-Publication Data

Names: Slade, Suzanne. | Lanan, Jessica, illustrator.
Title: Out of school and into nature : the Anna Comstock story /
written by Suzanne Slade ; illustrated by Jessica Lanan.
Description: Ann Arbor, MI : Sleeping Bear Press, [2017] |
Audience: Age 6-10.
Identifiers: LCCN 2016026786 | ISBN 9781585369867
Subjects: LCSH: Comstock, Anna Botsford, 1854-1930—Juvenile liter-
ature. | Naturalists—United States—Biography—Juvenile literature.
| Women naturalists—United States—Biography—Juvenile literature. |
Natural history—Juvenile literature.
Classification: LCC QH31.C72 S53 2017 | DDC 508.092—dc23
LC record available at https://lccn.loc.gov/2016026786